AMONG THE FLOWERING REEDS

Among the Flowering Reeds

CLASSIC KOREAN POEMS
WRITTEN IN CHINESE

EDITED & TRANSLATED BY
KIM JONG-GIL

WHITE PINE PRESS • BUFFALO, NEW YORK

Publication of this book was made possible, in part, by grants from the
Korean Literature Translation Institute and from the Witter Bynner
Foundation for Poetry.

Published under agreement with Anvil Press Poetry, London, England.

First Edition

Printed and bound in the United States of America.

ISBN 1-893996-54-9

Library of Congress Control Number: 2003100353

Published by White Pine Press
P.O. Box 236, Buffalo, New York 14201

www.whitepine.org

Contents

Preface

THIS ANTHOLOGY of one hundred classical Korean poems in Chinese covers a period of over a thousand years from the late ninth century to the end of the first decade of the twentieth. The majority of the poets included are represented by only one poem each; a dozen poets by two; and only two poets by as many as three. Poets are arranged in the chronological order of the dates of their birth, but where those dates are uncertain or unknown, the arrangement is necessarily conjectural.

The project out of which this book has evolved began a number of years ago. The work was extremely time-consuming, especially since it involved the maintenance of a precarious balance, a sort of tightrope-walking, between two shaky poles. I mean, of course, the challenge of translating from Chinese to English, both of which languages I have acquired only by study. Needless to say, the more difficult part of the venture has been to make readable English versions with a maximum of both linguistic and poetic fidelity to the originals. It has entailed an almost endless process of revising and testing the drafts on such native speakers of English as I have been able to consult.

To bring out more saliently the Korean character of this particular genre, I have chosen poems free from Chinese allusions, and in making my selection I have also been guided to a certain extent by their popularity in Korea. Classical Chinese in poetic forms is inherently concise and terse, often requiring in translation a change of the original syntax or a sacrifice of the original sense and imagery. So I have taken some liberties with the literal sense of the original at times for the sake of poetic accuracy or rhythmic balance in the translated version. I have also used compression in translating the titles of some poems, when they are so specific that it hardly seems necessary to render them literally.

In preparing this slim volume, I am indebted to a number of people for their help; but my special thanks are due to Professor Yi Tong-hwan for his kind explanations of points in the originals I inquired into; to Dr. Rob Wilson for his patient reading of my first drafts; and to the late Sir William Empson for his magnanimity in preparing a dozen sheets of invaluable comments and suggestions regarding the versions I showed him in July, 1983. It must have taken him many hours during that unusually hot spell in London nine months before his death. That, among other things, is why I dedicate this volume to his memory. And last but not least, I express my gratitude to the Korean Culture and Arts Foundation for its grant and encouragement which enabled me finally to complete this long and delicate undertaking.

In this revised editon of *Slow Chrysanthemums* (Anvil Press Poetry, London, 1987) translations have been revised and the dates of the poets corected and made considerably more accurate. The Chinese texts have been omitted and short biograhical notes have been added for each poet. Thanks are due to Dennis Maloney of White Pine Press for making this anthology readily available to the reading public.

—Kim Jong-gil

Introduction

UNTIL THE EARLY days of this century, poetry-writing in classical Chinese was very much a part of the life of an educated Korean. Chinese versification was regarded as an important discipline for Korean students in former times, a discipline at once aesthetic and moral. They studied Confucian texts and histories and literary works of ancient China, and were also made to memorize masterpieces of Chinese poetry and prose. Of the poetic texts they learned, *Shi-ching* (the Confucian Anthology) and the representative works of T'ang poets were indeed indispensable. Not only did they have to memorize them; they were also made to compose in the same forms and on the same models they had learned by heart. The test of their attainment was often whether they could write decent verse in Chinese and a scholarly reputation could depend, almost exclusively, on the quality of one's writing in the Chinese medium and meters. Thus in Korea in past ages, most scholars were poets and most poets were scholars.

All this, however, does not mean that the Korean people had no language of their own. On the contrary, they had a native language distinct from Chinese in all its linguistic features, but no systematic means of writing it down. This is the reason why they adopted Chinese characters and why classical Chinese remained the primary written language in Korea for such a long period. So deep-rooted, indeed, was this foreign medium in Korean intellectual life that when *Hangul*, the phonetic Korean alphabet, was invented and promulgated in the mid-fifteenth century it was virtually ignored and even despised by Korean scholars. For them the new writing system was too simple and too easy to learn, and it took over four hundred years for *Hangul* to replace Chinese in official and general use. In the meantime, it was used mostly by the womenfolk of the upper-class and by certain literati when they tried their hands at writing Korean language verse and prose. It is indeed small wonder that, up to the beginning of this century, the quantity of Korean poetry written in Chinese overwhelmed that of Korean poetry in its native language.

Brought up as a child in a Confucian family of a traditionally most learned milieu in Korea, I still remember clearly how the older members of my family devoted their lives to the study of Chinese and Chinese-language Korean classics and how much they loved to read and write in classical Chinese. I often had a chance to watch them having a "poetry gathering" with their friends and relatives, either at home or at a country "pavilion." At such a gathering, they used to agree first on a common subject and a common set of "rhyme characters" before they went on composing in their heads. Some sat cross-legged on the floor, gently swaying their bodies from side to side; some stood, their hands clasped at the back of their waists, looking at a far-away corner of the sky or mountains; and some loitered in the garden or by a stream, humming to weigh the sounds and senses of Chinese words and phrases. When the poems were completed, they were written down, by dictation, in beautiful calligraphy on a "poetry scroll" and appreciated by being chanted one after another.

Meanwhile comments would be made on the poems and sug-
gestions proposed to improve them, and then the whole event
would end up with food and drinks.

Such gatherings were by no means the only occasions for
writing poems for Korean scholars in earlier times; they took,
in fact, almost every opportunity to compose them. They
often sent poems to their friends, who replied in turn with
poems employing the same rhyme schemes used in the poems
sent to them. They wrote a variety of occasional poems—
commemorative, congratulatory, and elegiac—in addition to
poems that were lyrical, descriptive, reflective, and even satir-
ical. The frequent casualness of the titles they used, such as
"Written on the Wall of a Monastery," "Written at Leisure,"
and "An Incidental Poem," attest to the fact that their poems
could be prompted by numerous passing moments of their
lives. They were, however, never published in their lifetimes;
they went around only in manuscripts and in copies. As in
Elizabethan England, there was a notion of the "vulgarity of
print" among the Korean poets of old times: their works were
printed only after their deaths, and even then only if of suffi-
cient merit and if their descendants could afford to defray the
expenses.

The first piece of Korean poetry that has been handed
down is a little lyric from Koguryŏ, an ancient Korean king-
dom which spanned the greater part of the Korean peninsula
and Manchuria from 37 B.C. to 668 A.D. According to old
records, the song was sung by Yuri, the second king of
Koguryŏ, in the early first century when he had been deserted

by his favorite concubine.

> Flutter, flutter the orioles,
> Male and female, together.
> But O, I am alone:
> With whom shall I go home?

Another celebrated poem from Koguryŏ is one of historical and military interest. It is a poem written by General Ŭlchi Mundŏk as a stratagem when the army of Emperor Yang of Sui invaded Korea in the early seventh century. Having lured the enemy forces into the outskirts of P'yŏngyang, the general, under the guise of surrender, sent the poem to Yu Chung-wen, a General of the Sui army.

> Your godlike plans plumbed the heavens,
> Your subtle reckoning spanned the earth.
> You have won the battle, and made your name:
> Then, why not be content and withdraw?

It was, however, in the late eighth century in the kingdom of Silla (53 B.C.–918 A.D.) that Korean poetry in Chinese attained a high level. Ch'oe Chi-wŏn, the greatest poet of the kingdom, went to China in 868, passed the T'ang civil service examination and held a number of official posts in China. He also became well-known as a poet, his works being published in one of the T'ang anthologies. His poem "On a Rainy Autumn Night" was presumably written in China, but another poem of his, "In My Study," belongs to his later years when he was back in Korea and had retired to the mountains in the last years of Silla. His contemporary Ch'oe Kwang-yu also studied in China, and his poem "On a Spring Day in Chang-an" reveals his homesickness and frustration during his study abroad. These poets, like most poets of later generations who wrote in Chinese, were Confucian scholars and officials. Ch'oe Ch'i-wŏn, however, set another precedent for a number of later poets by being at the same time deeply connected with Buddhism. Mount Kaya, to which he retired in his later years is, in fact, the site of Haein-sa, one of the important Buddhist temples of the Silla period.

The subsequent kingdoms of the Koryŏ and Yi Dynasties also saw a great flowering of Chinese-language poetry. It was written not only by Confucian scholars and statesmen, but also by Buddhist monks and masters. During the Koryŏ period (918–1392), Wŏngam was Buddhist, as was Ch'oe Hang before he came to power in succession to his father, Ch'oe U. Some Confucian poets of the period also leaned conspicuously toward Buddhism: prominent among them were Kim Pu-shik, who was also a great historian, and Yi Il-lo, who was the first remarkable Korean critic as well as being an outstanding poet of the era. Even Yi Kyu-bo, a great man of letters and Confucian statesman of Koryŏ, has such a distinctly Buddhist poem as "The Moon in the Well." Yi Saek, who, like his father, served as an official in the Yüan and the Koryŏ dynasties, almost became a Buddhist in his later years and after the fall of the Koryŏ Dynasty. It is true that during the

Koryŏ period Buddhism exerted a great influence on national life; but the Yi Dynasty (1392-1910) was predominantly Confucian. This great Confucian era, however, did not lack in Buddhist poets. Hyujŏng, the Great Master of Sŏsan, who led thousands of warrior-monks against the Japanese invasion near the end of the sixteenth century, is perhaps the greatest among them. And again, such a Confucian poet as Kim Shi-sŭp, who was one of King Tanjong's "six loyal subjects who survived," in fact lived as a Buddhist monk for many years.

A remarkable fact about the Yi Dynasty period is that it produced a number of talented women poets who wrote in Chinese. It is remarkable because, in those days when women were seldom given formal education, they educated themselves in Chinese and in its rigid versification. Some of them, such as Shin Saim-dang, the celebrated mother of the eminent scholar-official, Yi I, and Hŏ Ch'o-hi, better known by her pseudonym Nansŏl-hŏn, were formidable ladies from respected upper-class families; others, perhaps greater in number, were not. Hwang Chin-i is a typical case, being simply a *kisaeng,* the Korean counterpart of a Japanese *geisha.* It was, however, her low social status that allowed her to write poems explicitly concerned with love, a subject largely taboo for Confucian poets of the upper-class. Such were Sŭng I-kyo, Yi Ok-bong, Kyewŏl and Nŭngun, as well as Hwang Chin-i, all of them being either *kisaengs* or concubines. Similarly, lower-class poets are also found among men of the period, such as Song Ik-p'il and So Han-p'il, Ch'oe Ki-nam and

Chŏng Pong. The brothers Song Ik-p'il and Song Han-p'il were born of a mother who was a slave, and Chŏng Pong was once a servant in an upperclass household. Kim Pyŏng-yŏn, usually known as Kim Satkat ("big hat woven with bamboo-shreds"), came from a disgraced, upperclass family and, deprived of the hope of a respectable career, made himself a tramp, often begging meals and improvising sarcastic poems.

These socially-underprivileged poets, however, suffered no literary discrimination; their poetry, in fact, was loved and admired the more for their plight in society. So was, and indeed still is, the poetry of such poets as Chŏng Mongju, Sŏng Sam-mun, Yi Sun-shin and Hwang Hyŏn, but for different reasons. These are poets who have been particularly admired by the Korean nation, for they embraced causes dear to them at the cost of their lives. Chŏng Mongju, a great scholar-official, refused, near the end of the Koryŏ Dynasty, at the risk of his life, to cooperate with Yi Dynasty founder Yi Sŏng-gye in order to remain loyal to his own dynasty. Sŏng Sam-mun, another of King Tanjong's "six loyal subjects who died," was killed for his part in an attempt to restore the king who had been forced to abdicate his throne. Yi Sun-shin, a famous Korean admiral who invented the world's first iron-clad vessel, is also respected for his unselfish dedication to the defense of the country against the Japanese invasion and for his superb naval tactics. And Hwang-Hyŏn was a distinguished poet and intransigent critic who killed himself in protest of Japan's annexation of Korea in 1910. Thus it is quite natural that, at least for Korean readers, the integrity of these poets should enhance the poignancy of their poetry.

As has been stated, almost all the educated in Korea were poets in those days; for them poetry was indeed a "superior amusement," as T.S. Eliot once defined it, recording their actual experiences and expressing their real feelings. Traditionally in China and Korea, poetry was believed to be *yen-chi,* "the utterance of what is in one's mind." Thus it was usually of a highly personal kind, admitting almost no distinction between the poem and the poet. It was regarded as a direct expression of the poet's own self and, therefore, as the spontaneous reflection of feelings, sentiments and attitudes in his actual life. As has also been mentioned, it was an important personal discipline vital to the formation of one's character, as is suggested by Confucius's frequent and almost pragmatic reference to the use of poetry in his *Analects* and elsewhere. So deep-seated in the ancient Eastern mind was this belief in the proximity between poetry and its author that it was often thought to be prophetic of his destiny. This Eastern version of the Roman concept of the poet as *vates* gave rise to the notion that a poem, often a very clever one, could prove fatal to the poet. In Korea, such a poem used to be called a *tanmyŏnghu,* literally a "life-shortening poem," which young scholars were warned against writing. This and similar Confucian scruples, it seems, have been operative in determining the general temper of classical Eastern and Korean poetry.

For Western readers, Korean poetry in Chinese might not

appear strikingly distinct from traditional Chinese poetry, just as the facial features of the Koreans are, for them, hardly distinguishable from those of the Chinese. It is, however, only natural that it should read like Chinese poetry, because it is in the same medium and forms and on roughly the same subjects. Its themes and sentiments are, of course, various: joys and sorrows; loneliness and nostalgia; self-mockery over one's vanity and misfortune; and even pathos in the face of one's own death. These themes and sentiments are almost invariably treated and expressed in and through natural backgrounds: mountains and valleys; streams and rivers; the moon, rain, wind, grass, trees and flowers. Consequently, the world embodied in it resembles the typical scene in traditional Eastern paintings with leisurely, detached people occupying a small space in a corner or in the foreground of a landscape of misty mountains, rivers and lakes. Poetry, however, is not painting; thanks to language, it can reveal man's states of mind in the flux of time with greater explicitness and intelligibility. It also can play upon ideas and logic to an extent that no other art can match in intellectual perspicuity. Whatever the setting and situation, therefore, a poem has its own specific human aspect based on its intellectual and emotional content. It is particularly in this human aspect of Korean poetry in Chinese that one may hope to come to grips with the elusive subject of its Koreanness.

It still remains very difficult, however, to draw a feasible distinction between traditional Chinese poetry and classical Korean poetry written in Chinese. Almost all the themes and sentiments of the latter are found in the former in almost exactly the same manner. Hence, such differences as there may be between the two are to be discovered not so much in their typical properties as in the degree to which such properties occur. Readers may notice at once the frequent appearance of mountains in Korean poetry in Chinese, while they will but rarely encounter in it the great rivers and expansive lakes which frequently appear in its Chinese counterpart. This difference, of course, derives from the geographical difference between China and Korea, and it is perhaps too obvious a feature to deserve dwelling upon. So let it suffice to consider here only one aspect of Korean poetry written in Chinese which seems to characterize it in an important way: the marked propensity of the poets to withdraw from the world, a propensity which often involves a kind of philosophical transcendence.

This tendency is by no means peculiar to the Korean poets, deriving partly from the prevalent instinct in traditional Eastern poets and philosophers, famously exemplified by T'ao Ch'ien (372-430) in his poem "Words on Returning Home." In classical Korean poetry, however, this tradition of withdrawal is especially prominent and has a specific historical significance as a reflection of the social conditions in which the poets found themselves. The world they lived in was a turbulent one that made them constantly desire to transcend it. Their love of nature and of the leisurely life, their acquiescence in anonymity in "clean poverty," and their scorn for vanity and worldly power all derive from this same desire.

It was their ideal to live in detachment from all the vulgarities and conflicts of the world by being as assimilated into nature as possible. All this may seem to suggest a mere escapism or even defeatism, and it would be difficult to assert that it was entirely free from such things. But there was another more significant side to it which differentiated it from a mere retreat of the defeated. Korean Confucians, especially those neo-Confucians of the Yi Dynasty, tended to be so austere in their principles that they were continually divided into tenacious factions on social, political, and even theoretical matters. Thus during the Yi Dynasty, in particular, Korean society was very factious, so much so that sensible scholars and poets had to try constantly to stand aloof from its wrangles. It was a significant token of their wisdom that they chose to turn away from the mess and muddle of the world.

Their fear of getting involved in violent social strife often achieves poetic transcendence primarily through robust and graceful irony. Even the seemingly straightforward "fear" of "disputes over right and wrong" in Ch'oe Ch'i-wŏn's poem "At My Study on Mount Kaya" turns out to be not as simple as it might first seem. In fact, it contributes to an affirmation of his positive stance toward the world because it is not so much the cause of his retiring from the world as the justification for his choice of the magnificent landscape where the mountain stream's "frenzied rush through the rocks roars at the peaks." This jaunty stance justifies the almost presumptuous assumption on the part of the poet, "I have arranged the waters to cage in these mountains."

A similar kind of robust irony may be found in the poets of much later ages as well. Yun Sŏn-do, a great seventeenth century poet who wrote in both Korean and Chinese, belonged to the faction of the "Southern Men," largely out of power in the latter half of the Yi Dynasty. His poem "In My Study," in spite of its ostensible detachment and nonchalance, conceals a heart seething with political passion. He begins the poem with an apparent indifference to the world: "My eyes fixed on the mountains and my ears on the lute, / How could affairs of the world ever disturb my mind?" This, again, is ironical, because the poet suggests that his proclaimed peace of mind is only apparent, and this in turn implies that there is something that causes him to struggle with himself. In reality, his mind is being very much disturbed by "affairs of the world," though he pretends it is not. That is why he declares with deliberate buoyancy that "Though nobody knows I am full of lively spirits, / Wildly I sing out a song, and then intone it alone." Another poet of the same century, Song Shi-yŏl, a great scholar and the leader of a faction called the "Old Arguers," then in power, plays upon a similar irony in a different direction. His poem "Going Up to the Capital" shows a paradoxical reflection on the occasion of his going into politics and power. Even at the moment of excitement, the poet contemplates the reverse side of its significance, finding that even the waters and mountains hate his "going into the wind and dust."

This dialectic of paradoxical irony, or double vision, attains a remarkable elegance and subtlety in such later poets as Yi Sang-jŏk, Kim Pyŏng-yŏn and Kang Wi. Yi Sang-jŏk, a noted poet and calligrapher who served as a local magistrate, has a satirical poem, "On the Roadside Monument." The subject of the poem is a monument erected to extol the former chief of a county who was, in fact, notorious for his avarice and cruelty while in office. It was an old and often hypocritical Korean custom to erect such a memorial stone to honor a former local magistrate, a practice which provided his successor with a chance for further extortion and corruption. Thus in this poem, the poet speaks tongue-in-cheek: "The piece of stone is speechless at the roadside: / How can the new magistrate compare with the old?" What he really means by implication is, of course, that neither the old nor the new official is really entitled to such an honor. Kim Pyŏng-yŏn was, as has been mentioned, a tramp-poet, and his poem "To an Ungenerous Host" was prompted by his being treated humiliatingly at a house where he begged a meal. The meal of gruel he was given in the yard, not in the house, was so thin and watery that it reflected "the sunlight and the wandering clouds." But he pretends to be high-minded, and so he is, in a sense, when in telling the mean host not to be ashamed of himself, he adds: "I love to see the mountains come imaged in water."

This gallant feat of poetic simulation achieves, through a sardonic irony, a transcendence of his humiliation and personal misery. A similar dialectic is found in Kang Wi's poem "On My Way to Such'un," in which the poet laments his own destitution and appears to be indulging in self-pity when he says: "Alas! I am poorer than the willows on the long riverbank."

But here again the poet rises elegantly above his misery and self-pity by comparing himself with the willows which have already shed their cotton-like catkins, changing their dress into a spring garment of green. It is through this paradoxical identification of the poet himself with the natural phenomenon that he is able to overcome his own situation.

Such an intimate relationship between the poet and nature may readily be perceived even in the necessarily brief selection of poems that it has been possible to consider here. Five of every six poems are related to nature in one way or another, and this in itself bespeaks the preponderance of nature in classical Korean poetry in Chinese and, indeed, in traditional Eastern poetry. It might well be called a "nature poetry" as a whole, but in a quite different sense from that associated with the poetry of Wordsworth. Nature in traditional Chinese or Korean poetry is not so much a partner of the poet with whom he holds communion as the very ambience of his life and poetry. He is indeed one with nature; and, as we have seen, albeit briefly, he has been capable of overcoming his pain and misery through it.

—Kim Jong-gil

Among the Flowering Reeds

On a Rainy Autumn Night

I sing a bitter song in the autumn wind,
with very few who really appreciate it.
Outside the window drips midnight rain:
under the lamplight, my thoughts drift far away.

Ch'oe Ch'i Wŏn
857 - ?

At My Study on Mount Kaya

The frenzied rush through the rocks roars at the peaks
and drowns out the human voices close by.
Because I always fear disputes between right and wrong
I have arranged the waters to cage in these mountains.

Ch'oe Ch'i Wŏn

On a Spring Day in Chang-an

I can't shake the street dust from my hemp clothes;
at dawn, I see in the mirror a face with a grey beard
       and wrinkles.
The flowers here are gorgeous but I am sad:
the trees of my old garden green in my dreams.
Oh to drift over the sea, homeward under the hazy moon
with my poor horse. I'm sick of asking which ford to cross.
I failed to study hard and now
I'm hurt by even the song of orioles in the willows.

Ch'oe Kwang-yu
9th to 10th century

Song of Cold Pine Pavilion

The moon stands white above Cold Pine Pavilion;
autumn waves are calm on Mirror Lake.
Listen to the sad cries coming and going:
friendly gulls along the sand by the sea.

Chang Yŏn-u
? - 1015

The Taedong River

After rain, the grass is lush along the riverbank.
Seeing you off at the ford, I burst into sorrowful song.
When will the waters of Taedong River be exhausted?
Year after year, tears of separation add to its green waves.

Chŏng Chi-Sang
? - 1135

At the Kamno-sa Temple

To where the vulgar do not come
I have climbed and feel serene.
The mountains look better in autumn;
even at night the river gleams.
White birds fly up and are gone;
the sailing boat goes lightly, alone.
Half my life I've spent, to my shame,
in this small world coveting fame.

Kim Pu-Shik
1075 - 1151

At an Inn in Kǔmyang-hyǒn

Dawn birds twitter in the frosty forest;
wind breaks the traveler's sleep.
The crescent lingers over the eaves,
and I am all alone at the edge of the sky.
Fallen leaves hide my path home:
last night's smoke hangs on cold boughs.
My home lies far to the west of the river,
and in this riverside village, autumn ends.

Ko Cho-ki
? - 1157

Written on the Wall of a Monastery

I waited for a friend, but he didn't come,
I looked for a monk, but he wasn't there.
Only a bird from beyond the forest
cordially invited me to have a drink.

Yi Il-lo
1152 – 1220

Night Rain on the River Hsio-hsiang

A stretch of blue water between the shores of autumn;
wind sweeps light rain over a returning boat.
As the boat is moored at night near the bamboo,
each leaf rustles coldly, awakening sorrow.

Yi Il-lo

Traveling on a Winter Day

How many inns and stations have I passed,
since I left Nakchu alone at dawn?
I came on horseback through flurries of white snow,
counting, with my whip, the jumbled blue mountains.
The sun set beyond the sky, warning me to return;
the wind blew cold in the field, sobering my drunken face.
I wanted to stop overnight in a remote village,
but the gate had closed early at every house.

Im Ch'un
12th–13th century

The Moon in the Well

A monk coveted the moon in the well
and fished it up with water into a jar.
But back at the temple, he will find
when the jar tilts, the moon spills.

Yi Kyu-bo
1168 - 1241

To My Son Editing My Poems

I have always feared withering sooner than
       the grasses and trees,
but I find the volumes of my poor poems worse than
       nothing.
Who will know, a thousand years from now,
that a man named Yi was born in a corner of Korea?

                     Yi Kyu-Bo

Along the Upper Reaches of the Nakdong River

On the path winding through the mountains,
I stroll leisurely along the Nakdong River.
The deep grass is sprinkled with dew,
the pines are quiet; there is no wind.
The autumn water is green as a duck's head,
the morning mist red as a monkey's blood.
Nobody knows this idle traveler is only
an old poet in this larger world.

Yi Kyu-bo

Quatrain

The moon in my garden is a smokeless candle;
the reflection of hills in my room, a voluntary guest;
the pine trees improvise on their strings the unscored tunes:
I enjoy them alone, with no one to share.

Ch'oe Hang
? - 1024

Walking in the Field

Plum blossoms have fallen, the willows droop;
I pace up and down slowly in the mountain breeze.
Whispers are heard from the fisherman's closed house
and over the river pass green threads of rain.

Chin Hwa
12th to 13th century

An Old Fisherman

Heaven has never been generous to the old fisherman
and seldom sent fair weather to the rivers and lakes.
Don't laugh, old fisherman, at the rough human world:
you chose to put yourself among eddies and rapids.

Kim Kŭk-ki
12th - 13th century

At a Station House

Through nearly fifty years in the lifespan of a man,
I have had little luck with my ill-fated career.
What have I achieved these years away from home?
I have returned empty-handed from so far away.
Still the forest birds warble kindly to me;
the wildflowers, wordless, smile to make me stay.
But the devil of poetry always nags at me;
together with poverty, it is the root of all my grief.

Kim Kŭk-ki

Written at Leisure

I raise the screen to let in the hue of hills
and connect a bamboo pipe dividing the stream's sound.
Few have come here all through the morning;
there is only a cuckoo calling his own name.

Wŏngam
1226 - 1292

After Snow in the Mountains

The paper quilt grows cold, the temple light dim;
the novice has not rung a bell all through the night.
He will start grumbling if I open the door so early,
but I have to see the garden's pine laden with snow.

Yi Che-hyŏn
1287 - 1367

A Love Song

Under the willow by the stream where I rinsed my silk,
a gallant young man whispered to me, clasping my hand.
Rain has dropped from the eaves for three months;
how can I bear to wash my fingers where his scent remains?

Yi Che-hyŏn

To A Friend

On a small boat, my lifelong wish unattained,
I return home, hair already white, laughing at myself.
Still I dream of service at the Emperor's court
and forget that I am now among the flowering reeds.

Yi Kok
1298 - 1351

Written on a Volume by a Friend

The path runs aslant, deep among the jumbled mountains;
at sundown, cattle find their way home on their own.
This is indeed the wish of an old man come true:
sweet grass, faintly misted, reaches to the sky.

Yi Saek
1328 - 1396

To My Husband at the Front

I have hardly heard from you in the years since you left:
I cannot be sure if you are alive.
This morning, I sent you some clothes against the cold;
the boy, in my womb when I saw you off, was in tears.

Chŏng Mong-ju
1337 - 1392

Visiting a Friend

Smoke, dim and faint, silhouettes the trees high and low;
grass covers up the trail, so one is likely to stray.
As I am still lost, though nearing your house;
an old farmer, without turning, points west of the bridge.

Chŏng To-jon

1342 - 1398

Visiting a Friend's Cottage

Autumn clouds are dreary over the hushed mountains:
falling leaves, soundless, crimson the ground.
I stopped my horse by the bridge to ask the way,
unaware that I stood in a scene from a painting.

Chŏng To-jon

A Monk's Hut

Where a track diverges north and south of the mountain,
pine pollen, soaked with rain, scatters.
The monk returns to his hut with water from a spring,
and a stretch of blue smoke colors the white cloud.

Yi Sung-in
1347 - 1392

On a Spring Day in the South of the City

Suddenly a spring breeze announces the season;
the fine rain still drizzles at day's end.
The apricot tree begins to burst at the corner of the house,
and some of its dew-wet branches bend toward me.

Kwŏn Keŭn

1352 - 1409

My Intention

Living alone under the thatched roof by a stream,
I am full of joy with the white moon and the fresh wind.
No guest comes, but the mountain birds are twittering;
I place my bed among the bamboo, lie down and read.

Kil Chae
1353 - 1419

At the Execution Ground

The beating drum presses for my life;
I turn and see the sun is about to set.
There is no inn in the nether world,
so at whose house will I sleep tonight?

Sŏng Sam-mun
1418 - 1456

Slow Chrysanthemums

The chrysanthemums are slow to bloom this year,
I have found no autumn joy by the eastern hedge.
Heartless, indeed, is the west wind: it blows
into my greying hair, not yellow chrysanthemums.

Sŏ Kŏ-jŏng
1420 - 1488

A Fisherman

Mountains rise over mountains and smoke from valleys;
the dust of the world can never touch the white gulls.
The old fisherman is by no means disinterested;
he owns, in his boat, the moon over the west river.

Sŏng Kan
1427 - 1456

Now Shine, Now Rain

Now shine, now rain, and rain becomes shine:
that is the sky's way, as well as man's.
My glory may well lead to my ruin;
your escape from fame will bring you a name.
Flowers may open or fall, but spring doesn't care;
clouds will come and go, but mountains do not argue.
Men of the world, you must remember
you won't find happiness where you crave joy.

Kim Shi-sŭp
1435 - 1493

Hearing a Nightingale

Since I left the imperial palace like a resentful bird,
I have dragged my lonely shadow among blue mountains.
I beg for sleep night after night, but sleep won't come;
year after year passes in grief, but the grief doesn't end.
Singing stopped, the moon is pale over the peaks at dawn;
blood streamed, fallen petals are red in the spring valleys.
When heaven is deaf to the song of a nightingale,
why are a grieving man's ears so keen?

Tanjong
1441 - 1457

My Way

I live in peace and quiet, confining myself to home;
only the moon is invited to shine on my loneliness.
Please don't ask me how I'm getting along:
there are endless misty waves and hills on hills.

Kim Koeng-p'il
1454 - 1504

On a Journey

At an edge of the sky, I grieve for my youth;
I long for home, but home is still far away.
As spring lets loose the wayward east wind,
no one owns the wild peach, but it bursts into bloom.

Kim An-guk
1478 - 1543

Written on the Wall of an Office

Illness may strike me, busy in my declining years;
even spring can hardly stir me to write poetry.
Waking from a nap, I am surprised to find
flowers fading and roses wet with rain.

Yi Haeng
1478 - 1534

Thinking of a Friend

Snow melts and swells the stream,
crows fly toward the clouds at dusk.
Sobered by the scene from drunkenness,
I write this poem and think of you again.

Pak Ŏn

1479 - 1504

Doing Nothing

All things change and all things remain the same,
I adapt myself at leisure to the flowing time.
As my strength has declined in recent years,
I look long at mountains but do not write poems.

Yi Ŏn-jŏk
1491 - 1553

To a Friend

At the gate of an old temple, another spring ends,
sprinkling my clothes with petals and rain.
As I return, sleeves full of the sweet fragrance,
innumerable mountain bees swarm after me.

Im Ŏk-nyŏng
1496 - 1568

On a Pond in Spring

The dewy grass softly, softly encloses the water
of a small pond, fresh and without a speck.
The pond is meant to mirror flying clouds and birds,
but I fear that swallows at times break its surface.

Yi Hwang
1501 - 1570

On Horseback

Going out in the morning, I stoop to hear the stream;
returning at dusk, I look up at the blue mountains.
Thus mornings and evenings are spent with mountains
      and water,
mountains like blue screens and water like a clear mirror.
In the mountains, I wish to dwell like a crane in the clouds,
by the water, to drift like a gull in the waves.
Wondering if government service has wrecked my life,
I boldly boast that I linger in a spirit land.

                                Yi Hwang

Looking Homeward from a Mountain Pass

Leaving my old mother in this seaside town,
alas, I am going to Seoul alone.
As I turn, once, to look homeward on my way,
white clouds rush down the darkening blue mountains.

Shin Saim-dang
1504 - 1551

Meeting in Dreams

My wish to see you is fulfilled only in dreams;
whenever I visit you, you visit me.
So let us dream again some future night,
starting at the same time to meet on our way.

Hwang Chin-i
16th century

Parting from a Lover

The paulownia in the garden sheds its leaves under
      the moon;
wild chrysanthemums yellow and wither in the frost.
In the pavilion that soars into the sky
we have gotten drunk over many a cup of wine.
Coldly the stream mingles with the sound of my lyre;
sweetly the "plum blossoms" drift through your flute.
We part in the morning, but my love will be forever
with you, my lord, over the distant blue waves.

Hwang Chin-i

Climbing a Mountain Peak

The myriad cities look small as anthills;
the brave by the thousands, maggots in a meat sauce.
Pillowed in serenity, as the moon catches a window,
I hear wind-tossed pines rustling irregular rhymes.

Hyu-jŏng
1520 - 1604

Boating at Dusk

Lost among flowers, the boat returns late;
expecting the moon, it drifts slowly down the shoals.
Though I'm drunk, I still drop a line:
the boat moves on, but not my dream.

Song Ik-pil
1534 - 1599

To the Moon

When on the wane, you are always impatient to wax,
but how do you so easily wane after waxing?
You are full only once in a month's thirty nights:
man's mind in a lifetime is exactly the same.

Song Ik-pil

An Incidental Poem

I have lived in the mountains for forty years,
safe from involvement in the broils of the world.
I relax leisurely at my cottage in the spring breeze,
with smiling flowers and willows dozing.

Sŏng Hon
1535 - 1598

On Resigning Office

Getting by depends not on man but on fate;
it wasn't my intention to always be on guard.
I have sent my resignation, left the king,
and taking a small boat, returned to the country.
My dullness is only fit for tilling the soil,
yet my dreams vainly hover around the palace.
Back at work in my thatched hut and stony fields,
I shall accept poverty for what remains of life.

Yi I
1536 - 1584

An Autumn Night

The rustling sound of falling leaves
I mistook for spattering rain.
I ordered a monk to go out and look;
he reports that the moon hangs on a bough.

Chŏng Ch'ŏl
1536 - 1593

Night at a Cottage

The moon fills the empty garden,
but where has the master gone?
Fallen leaves pile at the brushwood gate,
and wind-tossed pines murmur into night.

Chŏng Chŏl

Spring at Yongmun

Since spring may come to my window any time,
I roll up my screen early and let it down late.
Spring is at its peak at the mountain temple;
the returning monk passes the flowers, unaware.

Paek Kwang-hun
1537 - 1582

At Night on Hansan Isle

Autumn light darkens over the sea;
wild geese fly high in the cold air.
As I toss about anxiously in the night
moonlight catches my bow and sword.

Yi Sun-shin
1545 - 1598

Parting Without a Word

A pretty girl, fifteen years old,
was too shy to say a word to her lover.
Back home, she shuts the double gate
and weeps before the moonlit pear blossoms.

Im Che
1549 - 1587

Coming Home after a War

I couldn't bear being homesick,
so I prodded my donkey a thousand leagues.
Spring is in its prime as it used to be,
but I find no one in the streets.
A storm has swept over the whole land,
even the sun and moon are eclipsed.
Any prosperity that grew here is gone:
it is chaos like the dawn of the world.

Chang Hyŏn-gwang
1554 - 1637

A Poor Woman

The poor woman, full of tears, rattled the shuttle,
weaving material for her husband's winter clothes.
In the morning she cuts it down to pay the back taxes,
one taxman leaves—and another arrives.

Yu Mong-in
1559 - 1623

A Lady's Complaint

My silk dress soaked and stained with tears,
I miss you more as the grass greens again.
I have played a love song on my jewelled lute.
Rain beats the pear blossoms; I bolt the gate.

Hŏ Ch'o-hi
1563 - 1589

A Poor Girl

She is not an ugly girl;
she sews and weaves well.
Brought up in a poor family,
there's no matchmaker she knows.

When she holds her scissors,
her fingers are stiff with cold.
She makes wedding dresses for others;
but she always sleeps alone.

Hŏ Ch'o-hi

On a Monk's Poetry Scroll

Azaleas are blooming and swallows flying;
I wake up dazed from a nap beside my lute.
A monk comes, but does not talk of the world,
knowing I, too, want to live in the blue mountains.

Shin Hŭm
1566 - 1628

At the Grave of Chŏng Ch'ŏl

Leaves fall with rain in these vacant mountains;
silent is the graceful voice of a poet-minister.
Alas, I cannot offer you a cup this morning;
you had a song that foretold it, in the old days.

Kwŏn pil
1569 - 1612

On an Autumn Night

Wild geese trail cold shrieks
and pass beyond the mountain walls.
I awake from a lonely dream of you;
my window is lit by the autumn moon.

Sŭng I-kyo
16th century

An Incidental Poem

Flowers opened in the rain yesterday
and fell in the wind this morning.
What a pity that spring
should come and go in rain and wind!

Song Han-pil
16th Century

On an Autumn Night

I wake from a dream, beneath a moonlit window.
Unable to control my longing, I sing alone in bed.
Now I regret that I thoughtlessly planted that tree;
its rustling fills the garden with autumn grief.

Kim Yŏn-gwang
1524–1592

Waiting for a Lover

You promised to come, but you haven't.
The plum blossoms in the garden begin to fall.
Suddenly I heard a magpie chirp on a bough,
but I have made up my face in vain.

Yi Ok-bong
16th century

Sorrows of Separation

Sorrows of separation have become a disease in me
that cannot be healed by wine nor cured by medicine.
Under my quilt I weep, like water under ice
which flows day and night, though no one knows.

Yi Ok-bong

To a Lover

How are you getting along these days, my lord?
The moon shines at my window and I am sad.
Had I left footprints where I went in my dreams,
the stone path to your gate would have turned to sand.

Yi Ok-bong

At the Old Capital

The moonlit snow, the color of a former dynasty,
the cold bell, sound of the old country.
I stand pensively on the southern lookout;
clouds rise, at dawn, above the castle ruins.

Kwŏn Kap
16th - 17th century

A New Swallow

Laughing away, with nonchalance, at all human affairs,
I have closed my pine-twig gate in the spring rain.
But the newly returned swallow, outside the screen,
seems to provoke me, arguing right and wrong.

Yi Shik
1584 - 1647

In My Study

My eyes fixed on the mountains and my ears on the lute,
how could the affairs of the world ever disturb my mind?
Though nobody knows, I am full of lively spirits,
wildly I sing out a song, and then intone it alone.

Yun Sŏn-do
1587 - 1671

To a Friend Retired in the Country

I hear you have settled back in the old county of Yangju,
where you live in seclusion in the expanse of soft grass.
You may shun the sky under a big hat, riding a cow,
without turning toward Seoul even in the spring breeze.

Yun Hwŏn
1573 - 1627

A Mountain Home

A dog barks at the brushwood gate,
a white cloud wanders outside the window.
Who would come along such a stony path?
Only a bird warbles in the spring forest.

Hŏ Kyŏng-yun
1673 - 1646

On New Year's Eve

I drink late into the night, but cannot sleep:
the dawn bell rings, but I am just the same.
It's not that new year's eve won't return,
but it's only human to regret the year's turning.

Kang Paek-nyŏn
1603 - 1681

Going Up to the Capital

The green waters roar as if angry,
the blue mountains hush, as if frowning.
Musing on the mountains and waters I realize
they hate my going into the world of wind and dust.

Song Shi-yŏl
1607 - 1689

Elegy on Myself

I have never had my fill of even poor food,
so how could I hope for such dishes and cups on my death?
I have never had more than a cupful of drink,
so why should I expect to taste a morsel of meat?
I go out the gate of the capital city
to lie beneath the west hill in the field.
The wind in the forest sobs in sorrowful sounds;
the moon over the hills beams its sad light.
The world is a place for a short stay:
my real home is in the underworld.
Who knows if the joy of a skeleton
will go on and on, like heaven and earth?

Ch'oe Ki-nam
1586 - ?

Sitting at Night

A quiet valley with no one's footprints,
an empty garden lit by the moon.
Suddenly my dog barks and I know
a friend with a bottle is knocking at the gate.

Ŏm Ŭi-Gil
16th - 17th century

A Lady's Complaint

The autumn wind withers the green leaves,
tears wither the bloom of my face.
It's because of you that I have grown gaunt,
and you will cast me aside when you return.

Cho Shin-jun
1573 - ?

Passing the Old Capital

Darkening clouds over ruined battlements,
cold rain washes the desolate terrace.
The mountains are blue as of old,
but how many brave men have come and gone.

Kwŏn Tae-un
1612 - 1699

In the Alley

She skimmed and fluttered in silk stockings,
went through a double gate and never reappeared.
But the snow is kind enough to remain in the alley,
retaining her footprints beside the wall.

Kang Se-hwang
1731 - 1799

Looking into the Mirror on New Year's Day

Suddenly I discover more beard has grown,
through it adds nothing to my six-foot height.
My face in the mirror changes as the years go by,
but my heart remains as innocent as a year ago.

Pak Chi-wŏn
1737 - 1805

Parting from a Lover

My tearful eyes look at yours, tearful too;
my broken heart faces yours, also breaking apart.
I have read, in books, of the sorrow of parting,
but never dreamed that it would happen to me.

Kyewŏl
18th century

Lamenting Poverty

I set out to be happy with poverty,
but I find it difficult now that I am poor.
I lose my dignity when my wife sighs,
and I cannot be strict with starving children.
Even trees and flowers look lifeless;
poetry and books have no appeal.
The barley ripens by the hedge of the rich,
good enough only for the peasants to view.

Chŏng Yak-yong
1762–1836

Laughing to Myself

You may have grain, but nobody to eat it,
or worry about hunger, if you have sons.
To be promoted, you must become a fool,
while the talented cannot find a place.
A household can seldom enjoy perfect bliss,
and the best principles always collapse.
A miserly father always has a prodigal son;
an intelligent wife, a stupid husband.
When the moon is full, clouds often come;
when flowers bloom, the wind often blows.
This is the way of things.
So I laugh to myself, but nobody knows.

Chŏng Yak-yon

A Dream

The way home is a thousand miles;
an autumn night is even longer.
Ten times already I have been home,
but the cock has not yet crowed.

Yi Yang-yŏn
1771 - 1853

Written on a Cottage Wall

In a small cottage by a stumpy willow tree
a lonely couple live, both with white hair.
They have never gone beyond the path by the stream
for seventy years, with the corn in the ripening wind.

Kim Chŏng-hi
1786 - 1856

On Hearing, in Exile, of My Wife's Death

If I could have Yueh-lao appeal to the underworld
for us to change places in the next life,
I could make you know the sorrow I feel now
when I die, and you would be alive a thousand leagues away.

Kim Chŏng-hi

Autumn Festival (Ch'usŏk)

The widow, on the day of the autumn festival,
wails all day at her husband's grave.
In the field below, the rice is ripening
which they tended together, but now cannot share.

Chŏng Sang-gwan
19th century

On the Roadside Monument

Funds were extorted for the old magistrate's monument,
but who exploited the people and forced them away?
The piece of stone is speechless at the roadside:
how can the new magistrate compare with the old?

Yi Sang-jŏk
1804 - 1865

At an Inn

Equipped with only a staff on a thousand league journey,
I have seven pennies left; I say it's still a lot.
I tell these coins to remain deep, deep in my pocket,
but what shall I do at the inn when the sun goes down?

Kim Pyŏng-yŏn
1807 - 1863

To an Ungenerous Host

A bowl of gruel on a four-legged pine table
reflects the sunlight and the wandering clouds.
Don't tell me, Sir, that you are ashamed of yourself:
I love to see mountains reflected in water.

Kim Pyŏng-yŏn

On My Way to Such'un

Down below, the river reflects sky and greenery;
I drop my walking stick and fall asleep in the grass.
Alas, I am poorer than the willows along the riverbank,
Still in my quilted cotton garb, though spring wind has gone.

Kang Wi
1820 - 1884

Lodging in the Capital

On my way to the capital at sundown,
knotweeds blossom white in the autumn wind.
When I get drunk, I fall asleep at any house:
so, why do I need to ask whose?

Yi Chong-wŏn
19th - 20th century

The East Lake

The spring water of the east lake is a deep, deep blue;
white birds stand out on it in twos and threes.
When they fly away at the soft sound of an oar,
the lake fills with mountains in the evening sun.

Chŏng Pong
19th century

The Swing

The girl, fourteen years old but taller than me,
has learned to swing like a swallow flying.
As I dare not speak aloud from outside her window,
I scribble on a persimmon leaf and throw it to her.

Hwang O
19th century

Waiting for a Lover

He swore he would come at moonrise;
the moon has risen, but he isn't here.
Probably, where he lives, the mountains
are high and the moon is slow to rise.

Nŭngun
Presumably 19th century

In a Boat

Flowers were opening at the house where I spent the night;
this morning I cross a river afloat with petals.
Spring is busy like people, coming and going:
no sooner have I seen the flowers than I see them fall.

Anonymous woman
Presumably 19th century

Peach Blossom

In rain it opens and falls in wind.
How many days can we see the peach blossom?
This brevity is in the blossom's nature:
not that the wind has been cruel nor the rain kind.

Yi Ki
1848 - 1909

On a Great-Granddaughter's Death

Sick for seven years in a life of eight,
you must indeed be restful, lying dead.
But how sad it is that in tonight's snow
you part from your mother without feeling the cold!

Anonymous Woman
date unknown

Autumn Rain at a Remote Temple

The rain drizzles on Mount Diamond in September;
every leaf drips with the sound of autumn.
I have shed silent tears alone for ten years,
wetting my miserable cowl, but in vain.

Hyejŏng
date unknown

Hearing of a Disaster

Though River Han is hushed and Mount Pugak frowns,
high officials still swarm about the world.
Look at the lives of traitors in bygone times;
no one who sold the pass ever got killed.

Hwang Hyŏn
1855 - 1910

On Killing Myself

Growing old through all these turbulent years,
I have often come very close to ending my life.
But today truly I have no other choice:
a flaring candle lights up the dark blue sky.

Hwang Hyŏn

Notes on the Poems

Page 32: Mount Kaya is located in South Kyongsang Province. Toward the end of the Silla dynasty, the elderly poet retired to the mountain with its torrential gorge.

Page 33: Ch'oe Kwang-yu was a contemporary of Ch'oe Ch'i-wŏn, and like him studied in Chang-an, the capital city of the Tang Dynasty.

Page 34: The location of the Cold Pine Pavilion and the Mirror Lake is Kangnŭng, a city on the east coast of Korea. The poem is said to be a translated version of a Korean-language song.

Page 35: The Taedong River flows through P'yŏngyang.

Page 36: The Kamno-sa Temple was located in Kaesŏng, about forty miles north of Seoul.

Page 37: Kumyang-hyŏn is now the Kumhwa area of Kangwŏn Province.

Page 38: There is a bird called in Chinese "carrying a bottle."

Page 39: The Hsiao-hsiang, a river in southern China, was famous for its scenery. The poem was written in response to a picture drawn by a Sung painter.

Page 40: Nakchu is now Sangju in North Kyŏngsang Province.

Page 43: The Nakdong River flows south through North and South Kyŏng-sang Provinces. "As red as a monkey's blood" is an idiom in Chinese.

Page 44: This poem, formerly attributed to Ch'oe Ch'ung (984 – 1068), has recently been identified as being by Ch'oe Hang.

Page 48: Wŏngam was a monk.

Page 59: Sŏng Sam-mun was one of the six courtiers of King Tanjong who, when the king had been forced by his uncle Sejo to abdicate his throne, attempted his restoration. The attempt was detected and they subsequently were executed.

Page 60: In the Far East, the west wind is the autumn wind.

Page 63: Tanjong, the sixth king of the Yi Dynasty, succeeded to the throne at the age of twelve, but was made to abdicate after three years' reign and forced to kill himself in exile. In this poem, he finds his own likeness in a nightingale. Line six may be taken as a symbolic expression of the quality of the nightingale's song and also as reference to the cruelties which ensued from his abdication.

Page 74: "Plum blossoms" here is the name of a Chinese tune for the flute.

Page 82: Yongmun is the name of a place not far from Seoul.

Page 83: Yi Sun-shin is the famous Korean admiral who defeated the Japanese navy during the Japanese invasion of Korea near the end of the sixteenth century. His naval base was at Hansan Isle.

Page 90: Chŏng Ch'ŏl (1538 – 1593), a great poet and high official, has a Korean-language song, "Offering a Cup."

Page 94: In Korea, a magpie is said to herald a welcome guest.

Page 100: Yangju is a county east of seoul.

Page 104: It is a Confucian custom to offer food and wine to the dead.

Page 115: Yüeh-lao is the Chinese marriage goddess.

Page 116: Ch'usŏk is the traditional day in autumn when offerings are made at the graves of one's family members.

Page 119: This poem is said to have been occasioned by a humiliating meal a country squire gave to the poet in the yard of his house.

Page 120: Such'un is now Ch'unch'ŏn of Kangwŏn Province. The last line alludes to the fact that the spring wind has blown away the cotton-like catkins of the willows and changed the trees into spring attire.

Page 127: Only the poet's surname, Nam, is known.

Page 128: Mount Diamond, famous for its scenic beauty, is situated on the east coast of Korea, just north of the present demilitarized zone. Hyejŏng was a Buddhist nun.

Page 129: River Han and Mount Pugak are both located in Seoul. This poem was written when the poet heard of the treaty signed between Korea and Japan in 1905, by which Korea was made a Japanese protectorate.

Page 130: This is one of four poems the poet wrote on his suicide in protest of Japan's annexation of Korea in 1910.

Biographical Notes

Ch'oe Ch'i-wŏn - Poet-scholar of the last period of Silla. He went to China in 868 to study, passed the T'ang civil service examinations, and held official posts in China, where he also earned high repute as a man of letters. On his return to Silla, he moved from place to place as a local official until he retired to Mt. Kaya, where he spent the last days of his life.

Ch'oe Kwang-yu - Poet-scholar of the last period of Silla. He, too, went to China to study and passed the T'ang civil service examinations. Like Ch'oe Ch'i-wŏn, he was one of the "Ten Sages of Silla." His poems were published during the Koryo Dynasty and later.

Chang Yŏn-u - Scholar-official of the early period of Koryo. During the invasion of Khitans in 1011, he escorted King Hyonjong down to Naju and was appointed to high-ranking official posts for his service.

Chŏng Chi-sang - Scholar-official of the early period of Koryo. Born in Kaesong, he insisted that the capital be moved to Kaesong and that the king of Koryo should be called "Emperor." He was one of the "Twelve Great Poets of Koryo" and learned also in Buddhism and the philosophies of Lao-tzu and Chuang-tzu.

Kim Pu-shik - Scholar, historian and man of letters of the early period of Koryo. He edited *The History of the Three Kingdoms,* Korea's first authentic history. He authored more than twenty volumes, which did not survive as a whole. Portions are extant in anthologies of later periods.

Ko Cho-ki - Scholar-official of the middle period of Koryo. He was learned and accomplished in writing poetry. He passed the civil service examinations in the early days of King Yejong's reign and eventually became a high-ranking official.

Yi Il-lo - Scholar and man of letters of the middle period of Koryo. He was a prodigy from his childhood, excelling in composition and calligraphy. He was a Buddhist monk at one time but returned to secular life, serving as an official. He authored a volume of prose, *Jottings to Relieve Idleness* (1214), which has survived.

Im Ch'un - Man of letters of the middle period of Koryo. He tried many times to pass the civil service examinations, all in vain. Like Yi Il-lo, he was one of the "Seven Sages of the Sea Coast," and a collection of his work has survived.

Yi Kyu-bo - Scholar-official of the middle period of Koryo. He loved poetry, wine, and the lute so much that he was nick-named "The Master of Three Cravings." From a petty local post, he rose to high-ranking posts at the court. A large collection of his work has survived.

Ch'oe Hang - Scholar-official of the early period of Koryo. At twenty, he passed the civil service examinations and eventually became a high-ranking official. His devotion to Buddhism was so great that he volunteered to repair the pagoda of the Hwangryongsa temple in Kyongju and turned his residence into a Buddhist temple.

Chin Hwa - Scholar-official of the middle period of Koryo. He passed the civil service examinations in 1200 and served at the court. He excelled in writing poetry, his reputation being coupled with that of Yi Kyu-Bo. A collection of his work has survived.

Kim Kĕuk-ki - Scholar-official of the middle period of Koryo. He passed the civil service examinations early but did not receive appointment until the reign of King Myongjong. He enjoyed a great reputation as a writer and was said to have left 150 volumes of work, which did not survive.

Wŏngam - Zen Buddhist priest of the middle period of Koryo. He was deeply learned in literature, as well as in Tripitaka, and his poetry was reputed even among the Confucians of that time. He stressed the unity of Zen and teaching. A collection of his work has survived.

Yi Che-hyŏn - Scholar and man of letters of the later period of Koryo. He served six kings, starting with King Ch'ungson, during whose reign he spent some time in Beijing, where he made friends with the Chinese scholar Chao Meng-fu (1254 - 1322). Two of the volumes he authored have survived.

Yi Kok - Scholar and man of letters of the late period of Koryo. He passed the civil service examinations of Yuan in 1317 and served for some time at the Yuan court. He also served at the Koryo court on his return to Korea. A collection of his work has survived.

Yi Saek - Scholar and man of letters. Son of Yi Kok, he was one of the "Three Hermits" at the end of Koryo. Among his disciples were such distinguished scholars as Kwon Keun, Kim Chong-Jik and Pyon Kye-Ryang, who started the mainstream neo-Confucian scholarship of the Yi, or Chosun, Dynasty. A collection of his poetry and another of his prose have survived.

Chŏng Mong-ju - Scholar and man of letters toward the end of Koryo. He was also one of the "Three Hermits." He was first in the civil service examinations in 1360 and held distinguished posts at the court. He was assassinated in consequence of his opposition to Yi Song-gye, the founder of the Yi Dynasty. A collection of his work has survived.

Chŏng To-jŏn - Scholar, man of letters, and politician at the end of Koryo and in the beginning of Chosun. He helped Yi Song-gye found the Chosun Dynsty, which he consolidated theoretically, ideologically, and institutionally. He also participated in editing a history of Koryo. A collection of his work has survived.

Yi Sung-in - Scholar and man of letters toward the end of Koryo. He passed the civil service examinations in the reign of King Kongmin and led a successful official life. He was famous for his writing, which Yi Saek once commended as almost unrivalled, even in China. A collection of his work has survived.

Kwŏn Keŭn - Scholar and man of letters toward the end of Koryo and in the beginning of Chosun. He held distinguished posts at the court. He was deeply learned in neo-Confucianism and reputed as a writer. A collection of his work has survived.

Kil Chae - Scholar and man of letters toward the end of Koryo and in the beginning of Chosun. One of the "Three Hermits," he held an academic post after passing the civil service examinations in 1383 but soon retired to the country-side, where he engaged in study and teaching. There were many scholars among his disciples central to the neo-Confucianism scholarship of Chosun. A collection of his work survives.

Sŏng Sam-mun - Scholar-official of the early period of the Chosun dynasty. He was one of King Tanjong's six martyred subjects. A collection of his work survives.

Sŏ Kŏ-jŏng - Scholar and man of letters in the early period of Chosun. He passed the civil service examinations in 1444 and eventually rose to very high posts in the court. He drafted most of the important official documents of the time and took a leading part in editing administrative, historical, and geographical compendia and literary anthologies. Two volumes of stories survive, along with a collection of his poetry.

Sŏng Kan - Scholar and man of letters in the early period of Chosun. He passed the civil service examinations in 1441, but his official service was not long because he died young. He was remarkably erudite and versatile. A collection of his work survives.

Kim Shi-sŭp - Scholar and man of letters in the early period of Chosun. He was a prodigy in his childhood, but he started wandering throughout the country at a young age, being disappointed by Sejo's usurpation. He is one of King Tanjong's six unmartyred subjects. Staying in the "South Hill" of Kyongju, he wrote a work of fiction, *Keumoshinhwa*. A collection of his poetry survives.

Tanjong - The sixth king of the Chosun Dynasty. His throne was usurped by his uncle, Sejo, and he was sent into exile and eventually assassinated while still in boyhood.

Kim Koeng-pil - Scholar and man of letters in the early period of Chosun. Disciple of Kim Chong-jik, he was deeply learned in neo-Confucianism. Among his disciples were such distinguished scholar-officials as Cho Kwang-jo and Kim An-guk. During his service at the court, he was killed during political strife. A collection of his work survives.

Kim An-guk - Scholar official of the middle period of Chosun. A disciple of Kim Koeng-pil, he passed the civil service examinations in 1501 and rose to eminent posts at the court. He was also a reputed writer, translating agricultural, moral, and philosophical texts into vernacular Korean. A collection of his work survives.

Yi Haeng - Scholar official of the middle period of Chosun. He passed the civil service examinations in 1495, rising to eminent posts at the court, but died in banishment. He excelled at calligraphy, as well as in writing. A collection of his work survives.

Pak Ŏn - Poet-scholar of the middle period of Chosun. He was noted as a writer in his boyhood and became a high-ranking official's son-in-law. He held academic posts at the court, but he was banished during political strife and executed at the age of twenty-five. His bosom friend, Yi Haeng, edited and published a posthumous volume of his work.

Yi Ŏn-jŏk - Scholar official of the middle period of Chosun. Dismissed from office, he retired to his hometown, Kyongju, and concentrated on studying neo-Confucian philosophy.

Reappointed to a post at the court, he was later banished to a northern part of Korea, where he died. A collection of his work survives.

Im Ŏk-nyŏng - Scholar official of the middle period of Chosun. He passed the civil service examinations in 1525 and served as local magistrate. He was noted for his generosity and integrity and also for his literary talent. A collection of his work survives.

Yi Hwang - Reputedly the greatest neo-Confucian philosopher of Chosun. He passed the civil service examinations in 1534 and stayed in official service for a while before retiring into the countryside to concentrate on studying and teaching. Besides being a great philosopher, he also excelled in writing and calligraphy. His works are collected in the voluminous *Complete Works of Toegye* and his reputation as a master of neo-Confucian philosophy is now almost world-wide.

Shin Saim-dang - Woman of letters and calligrapher-painter of the middle period of Chosun. Mother of Yi I, a great scholar-official, she was admired as a paragon of the "wise mother and good wife." She excelled in writing poetry, calligraphy and painting.

Hwang Chin-i - Renowned *kisaeng* of the middle period of Chosun. Born in Kaesong, she was included in the "Three Beauties of Kaesong," along with the scholar So Kyong-doc and the Pakyon Waterfall. Though not many of her poems in both classical Chinese and vernacular Korean have survived, her reputation as a poet equalled that of Ho Ch'o-ji.

Hyu-jŏng - Renowned Buddhist priest and a leader of monk-warriors in the middle period of Chosun. Great Master of Sosan, as he was called, he led monk-warriors during the Japanese invasion, greatly contributing to recaputuring Seoul. He also advocated unification of Confucianism, Buddhism, and Taoism. An anthology of his work survives, as does one complete volume.

Song Ik-pil - Scholar and man of letters in the middle period of Chosun. Coming from a lower-class family, he rose to an eminent post at the court. He excelled in writing poetry and prose and was included in the "Eight Outstanding Writers" during the reign of King Sonjo. There were a number of distinguished scholars among his disciples. A collection of his work survives.

Sŏng Hon - Scholar of the middle period of Chosun. Through correspondence, he discussed moral philosophy with Yi I. A collection of his work survives.

Yi I - Scholar-official of the middle period of Chosun. He held many eminent posts at the court. Relieved from office, he retired to Haeju, where he concentrated on studying and teaching. With Yi Hwang, he was the representative

Confucian scholar of Chosun. He also excelled in writing poetry and his work is collected in the voluminous *Complete Works of Yulgok*.

Chŏng Ch'ŏl - Man of letters and politician of the middle period of Chosun. He was first in the 1562 civil service examinations and held many eminent posts, including that of prime minister. As a leader of his political faction, he was banished many times. An anthology of his work and one complete volume of his poetry survive.

Paek Kwang-hun - Poet of the middle period of Chosun. He studied under distinguished scholars, both in the countryside and in Seoul. He was one of three outstanding poets of his time and also noted for his calligraphy. A collection of his work survives.

Yi Sun-shin - Distinguished admiral of the middle period of Chosun. During the Japanese invasion, he built the Turtle Boat, the world's first iron-clad ship, vanquishing the Japanese navy. Author of *A War Diary*, he was killed in a naval battle.

Im Che - Man of letters of the middle period of Chosun. He passed the civil service examinations in 1577 and stayed in official service for a while. Disappointed at the factional strife at the time, he retired to the countryside, indulging in nature and poetry. Besides an anthology of his work, two complete collections survive.

Chang Hyŏn-gwang - Scholar of the middle period of Chosun. He declined official appointments and concentrated on studying neo-Confucian philosophy. A collection of his work survives.

Yu Mong-in - Scholar and man of letters of the Chosun middle period. He was first in the 1589 civil service examinations and held various posts at the court. Both he and his son were executed for political reasons. An anthology of his work, as well as a collection of short stories, survives.

Hŏ Ch'o-hi - Woman poet of the middle Chosun period. Coming from a talented family, she learned poetry from the poet Yi Tal, a family friend. She died at the age of twenty-six but authored two narrative poems in vernacular Korean, along with work in classical Chinese, which was collected in a volume that survives.

Shin Hŭm - Scholar and man of letters of the Chosun middle period. He was one of the "Four Great Writers in Classical Chinese" of that period. He passed the civil service examinations in 1586 and rose to the post of prime minister. A collection of his work survives.

Kwŏn Pil - Man of letters of the Chosun middle period. A disciple of Chong Ch'ol, he loved freedom and did not seek official employment. He died on his way to the place of his banishment, to which he had been exiled for writing a poem of political satire. One collection of his work survives.

Sŭng I-kyo - Renowned *kisaeng* of the Chosun middle period. She came from Chinju, South Kyongsang Province.

Song Han-pil - Scholar-official of the Chosun middle period. Like his brother, Song Ik-pil, he was a renowned scholar and poet. Yi I once said, "The Song brothers are the only scholars worth discussing neo-Confucian philosophy with." One collection of his work survives.

Kim Yŏn-gwang - Scholar-official of the Chosun middle period. He passed the 1555 civil service examinations and held a number of local posts. During the Japanese invasion, he defended his castle to the death. One collection of his work survives.

Yi Ok-bong - Woman poet of the Chosun middle period. Born of a local official's concubine, she, too, had to become a concubine, but she was also a respected poet of the time, rivaled only by Ho Ch'o-hi, both of whose poetry was published in China.

Kwŏn Kap - Scholar-official of the middle period of Chosun. Brother of Kwon Pil, he received an official appointment at one time.

Yi Shik - Scholar and man of letters of the middle period of Chosun. Descendent of Yi Haeng, he passed the 1610 civil service examinations and rose to various eminent posts at the court. He was also renowned for his writing and included in the "Four Great Writers in Classical Chinese." A collection of his work and a commentary on Tu Fu's poetry survive.

Yun Sŏn-do - Scholar and man of letters of the middle period of Chosun. He was first in the 1628 civil service examinations and held the posts of teacher to the princes, as well as other posts. He especially excelled at writing *shijo*, and was included in the "Three Great Shijo Poets" of Chosun. A collection of his work survives.

Yun Hwŏn - Scholar-official of the middle period of Chosun. Disciple of Song Hon, he passed the 1597 civil service examinations and held important official posts, along with his three brothers. He was executed for an offense he allegedly committed during the Japanese invasion.

Hŏ Kyŏng-yun - Man of letters of the middle period of Chosun. Recommended by a local magistrate, he once held a petty official post.

Kang Paek-nyŏn - Scholar-official of the Chosun middle period. He passed the 1627 civil service examinations and rose to an eminent post in the court. He was renowned for his integrity during his official service. One collection of his work survives.

Song Shi-yŏl - Scholar-official of the middle period of Chosun. Leader of a political faction, he was banished many times until he was ordered executed during his banishment on Cheju Island. A voluminous collection of his work survives.

Ch'oe Ki-nam - Man of letters of the middle period of Chosun. A commoner himself, he was admired by the upper-class literati, publishing, with other commoner poets, an anthology of poetry in 1660. One collection of his work survives.

Ŏm Ŭi-gil - Man of letters of the middle period of Chosun.. He came from Yongwol, Kangwon Province.

Cho Shin-jun - Scholar-official of the middle period of Chosun. He passed the 1649 civil service examinations and held local posts. He authored a volume of geography, *A Miscellany of Songdo* (Kaesong) which survives, as does a collection of his poetry.

Kwŏn Tae-un - Scholar-official of the late period of Chosun. He passed the 1649 civil service examinations and eventually rose to the office of prime minister. He was renowned for his frugality and integrity.

Kang Se-hwang - Man of letters of the late period of Chosun. A resident in Ansan, Kyoggi Province, he concentrated on learning, calligraphy and painting. By King Yongjo's favor, he began official service at the age of sixty. A master of poetry, calligraphy, and painting, he played a central role in the artistic circles of the time.

Pak Chi-wŏn - Scholar in *shilhak* (positivist learning) and man of letters of the late period of Chosun. He authored a travelogue, *Yolha Diary*, about his journey to China and was appointed to a local post in 1786. A collection of his work survives.

Kyewŏl - *Kisaeng* of the later period of Chosun. Coming from Pyongyang, she was said to be a beloved concubine of the eminent scholar-official Yi Kwang-dok (1690–1748).

Chŏng Yak-yong - Scholar in *shilhak* and man of letters of the late period of Chosun. Favored greatly by King Chongjo, he was in official service until he was banished in 1801. During his subsequent nineteen-year banishment in Kangjin, South Cholla Province, he authored numerous books on various subjects. They are collected in the encyclopedic *Complete Works of Yoyudang.*

Yi Yung-yŏn - Scholar-official of the later period of Chosun. He excelled in writing and in scholarship from his earliest days and held important official posts. A few complete volumes of his work, as well as an anthology, survive.

Kim Chŏng-hi - Scholar, man of letters, calligrapher and painter of the late period of Chosun. He passed the 1819 civil service examinations and held important official posts. He traveled to Beijing, where he became friends with the distinguished scholar Weng Fang-kang. He excelled in poetry, painting, studies in monument inscriptions, and especially in calligraphy. A collection of his work survives.

Chŏng Sang-gwan - Man of letters of the late period of Chosun.

Yi Sang-jŏk - Poet and calligrapher of the late period of Chosun. Coming from a family of interpreters, he traveled to China many times and got acquainted with a number of well-known Chinese men of letters. He studied under Kim Chong-hi and was learned in antiques and monument inscriptions, as well as in poetry. A collection of his work survives.

Kim Pyŏng-yŏn - Poet of the later period of Chosun. A wandering poet, he was nicknamed "Kim Satkat" (bamboo hat). Coming from a disgraced upperclass family, he took to wandering throughout the country, improvising humorous and satirical poems.

Kang Wi - Scholar and man of letters of the late period of Chosun. Coming from a family that was discriminated against, he gave up the civil service examinations and concentrated on learning and writing. He bacame a disciple of Kim

Chong-hi, who was in banishment on Cheju Island, and was an ardent admirer of enlightenment ideas through his two visits to China. A collection of his work survives.

Yi Chong-wŏn - He passed the civil service examinations in 1888 and held local official posts.

Chŏng Pong - Originally a servant of an upperclass family, he was a self-taught poet.

Hwang O - Poet of the last period of Chosun. He came from Sanju, North Kyonsang Province.

Nŭngun - *Kisaeng* of the later period of Chosun. Nothing is known of her life.

Anonymous Woman - Nothing is known of her life.

Yi Ki - Scholar and man of letters of the last period of Chosun. Believing in *shilhak*, he engaged in restoring national sovereignty and in patriotic enlightenment movements. A collection of his work survives.

Anonymous Woman - Her family name was Nam. Her father and husband were both said to be officials.

Hyejŏng - She was a Buddhist nun.

Hwang Hyŏn - Scholar, man of letters, and patriot of the last period of Chosun. When he was young, he made friends with eminent poets in Seoul. He passed the civil service examinations but he gave up official service, retiring into the countryside of Kurye, South Cholla Province, where he concentrated on writing. Upon Japan's annexation of Korea, he killed himself, leaving four poems on his suicide. Several historical records and a collection of his work survive.

The Korean Voices Series

Shrapnel & Other Stories
Selected Stories of Dong-ha Lee
Edited & Translated by Hyun-jae Yee Sallee
1-893996-53-0   176 pages $16.00

Brother Enemy: Poems of the Korean War
Edited & Translated by Suh Ji-moon
1-893996-20-4   176 pages $16.00

The Snowy Road: An Anthology of Korean Fiction
Edited & Translated by Hyun-jee Yee Sallee
1-877727-19-9   168 pages $12.00

A Sketch of the Fading Sun: Stories of Wan-suh Park
Edited & Translated by Hyun-jae Yi Sallee
1-877727-93-8   200 pages $15.00

Heart's Agony: Selected Poems of Chiha Kim
Translated by Won-chun Kim and James Han
1-877727-84-9   128 pages $14.00

Strong Wind at Mishi Pass: Poems by Tong-gyu Hwang
Translated by Seong-kon Kim & Dennis Maloney
1-893996-10-7   118 pages $15.00